SELENA &
♡ FOREVER FRIENDS

SCHOLASTIC INC.

New York   Toronto   London   Auckland
Sydney   Mexico City   New Delhi   Hong Kong

Cover: © Jean-Paul Aussenard/WireImage/Getty Images
Back Cover: © K Mazur/TCA 2008/WireImage/Getty Images
Interior: PG1: © K Mazur/TCA 2008/WireImage/Getty Images; PG4: © K Mazur/TCA 2008/WireImage/Getty Images; PG6: © Mark Savage/Corbis; PG9: © Hit Entertainment. Courtesy: Everett Collection; PG12: © Jean-Paul Aussenard/WireImage/Getty Images; PG15: © Andrew H. Walker/Getty Images; PG16: © AXELLE WOUSSEN/Bauer Griffin; PG18: © F Micelotta/TCA 2008/Getty Images for Fox; PG21: © David Fisher/Rex USA; PG23: © Chris Daniels/Retna Ltd.; PG24: © Picture Perfect/Rex USA; PG26: © AXELLE WOUSSEN/Bauer Griffin; PG29: © Dave M. Benett/Getty Images; PG30: © Brian Zak/Sipa Press/AP Photo; PG32: © Dimitrios Kambouris/WireImage/Getty Images; PG35: © Valerie Macon/Getty Images; PG36: © Frank Trapper/Corbis; PG38: © K Mazur/TCA 2008/WireImage/Getty Images; PG40 © AXELLE WOUSSEN/Bauer Griffin; PG42: © F Micelotta/TCA 2008/Getty Images for Fox; PG44: © 20th Century Fox/Everett/Rex USA

© 2009 by Scholastic
ISBN-13: 978-0-545-20030-1
ISBN-10: 0-545-20030-X

Published by Scholastic Inc.
SCHOLASTIC and associated logos are trademarks and/or registered trademarks of Scholastic Inc.

12 11 10 9 8 7 6 5 4 3 2 1   9 10 11 12 13 14/ 0

Designed by Deena Fleming
Printed in the U.S.A
First printing, September 2009

TABLE OF CONTENTS

INTRODUCTION

Have you and your best friend ever wondered what it would be like to be stars? To get to be in movies? Record albums? Go on tour? Or have your own television show? It would be awesome, right?

Well, two best friends get to do all of those things every day. Selena Gomez and Demi Lovato are some of the hottest new stars in Hollywood. But before they were stars, they were just two regular girls from Texas.

CHAPTER 1
TEXAS BEAUTIES

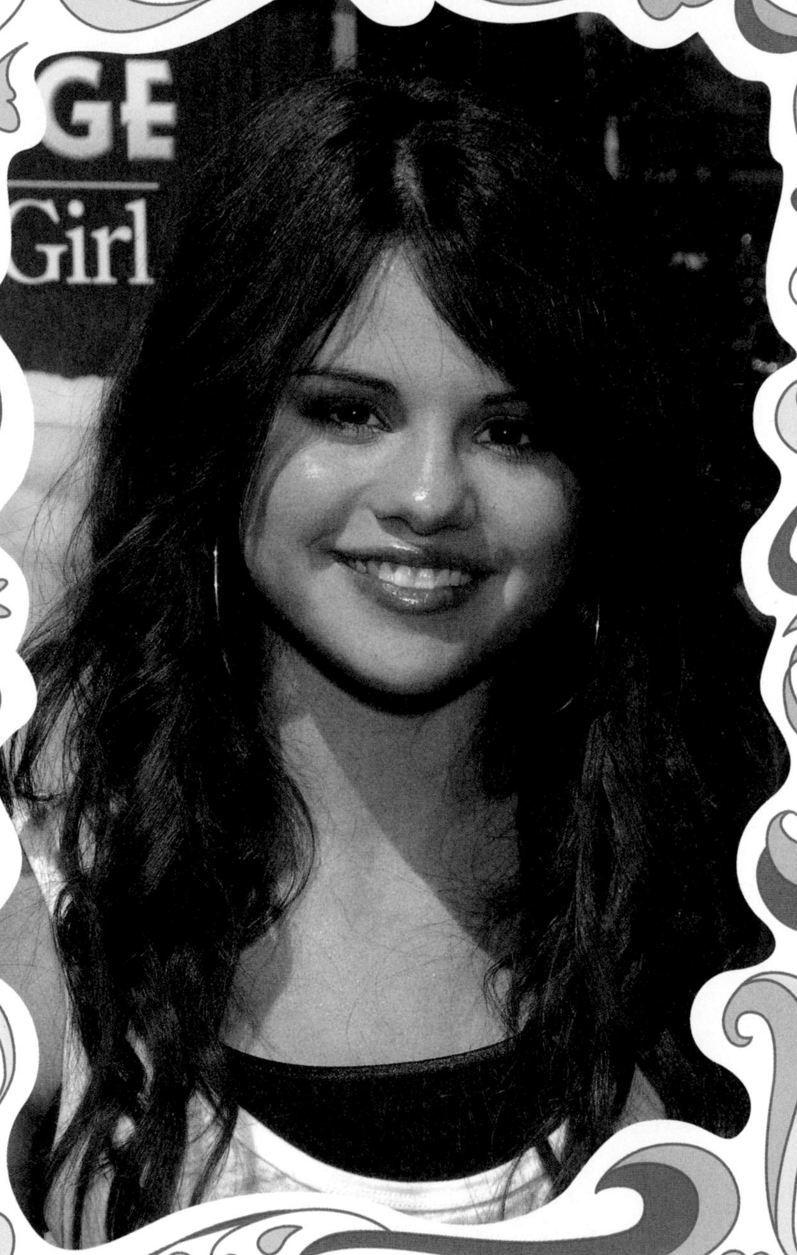

Selena Marie Gomez was born on July 22, 1992, in New York City. Her parents are Ricardo and Mandy Gomez. Sadly, Mandy and Ricardo got a divorce when Selena was five years old. But Selena and her dad are still close.

After the divorce, Selena and Mandy moved to Texas. They lived in a small town called Grand Prairie near Selena's grandmother's home.

Selena had lots of family in town. She also made new friends through school and sports. "I've had the same friends since kindergarten, so everyone is still really close," Selena told *Girl's Life* magazine. Selena spent lots of time outside with her friends and cousins. Her favorite sport to play was basketball.

Eventually, Selena's family grew. Her mom fell in love with a great guy named Brian Teefey. Mandy and Brian were married in 2006 when

Selena was 13 years old. Brian was a great addition to the family.

Even as a little girl, Selena had big dreams. Selena loved watching her mom act at the local theater. She knew that she wanted to be an actress, too. "My mom did a lot of theater when I was younger. I loved running lines with her, and then one day I tried out for something and got it, and it all started!" Selena told pbskids.org. The show that Selena tried out for was *Barney & Friends*. *Barney* was a television show about a big purple dinosaur who taught kids about manners. Selena met Demi on *Barney*.

Demi and Selena auditioned to be on *Barney* when Demi was six and Selena was seven. They even colored together while they waited in line to try out! They were nervous about going to such a big audition, but waiting together was fun.

"I was definitely nervous. . . . But then when I got to the audition, I realized it was just running lines, just like I always did with my mom," Selena told pbskids.org.

Luckily they both got jobs on the show that day. The two girls became BFFs while filming *Barney* for two years. They helped each other through lots of ups and downs. They also discovered that they had a lot in common.

Demetria Devonne Lovato was born in Dallas, Texas, on August 20, 1992. Her parents called her Demi for short. Her mother, Dianna was a country music singer. Demi's dad Patrick Lovato worked in construction. Sadly, Demi's parents divorced shortly after Demi was born. Patrick moved to New Mexico to be close to his family. But he talks to Demi often!

When Demi was five she was in her kindergarten talent show. From that moment

on, Demi knew that she wanted to be a singer or actress. Demi began going to acting, singing, and dancing classes. She also competed in beauty pageants and auditioned for commercials. Demi's big sis, Dallas, helped her get ready for auditions. The two sisters have always been very close. Later their mother re-married. She gave them a baby sister named Madison in 2002. Demi's stepfather is named Eddie De La Garza. Eddie is Demi's manager as well as her stepdad. Demi knows she's lucky to have such a supportive family behind her.

CHAPTER 2
CHASING THE DREAM

After they finished *Barney & Friends*, Demi and Selena looked for other jobs. They both took classes to improve their skills. And they went to lots of auditions.

Selena did several local commercials. Then, when she was 11 years old, she got a small part in *Spy Kids 3-D*. It was a very big movie, so Selena was excited. It was her first feature film. She was also in a television movie for the TV show *Walker, Texas Ranger*. Next, Selena landed the lead role in a show called *Brain Zapped*. It was a show for kids about how cool reading can be. It used lots of cool special effects. The show never made it to television, but it was really fun to film.

After that, Selena went to a Disney casting call. Disney was looking for talent, and they found it in Selena! The Disney Channel brought her to Los Angeles for more auditions. "They

flew us out to California. It was definitely scary," Selena explained to *Variety*. But Selena did very well and Disney began looking for parts for her on their shows.

Of course, Demi was keeping busy, too. She loved acting, but she also loved music. So, when Demi was eleven, she learned to play the piano and the guitar. She also started writing her own songs. She even recorded a few of them. Then she went on tour with big sis Dallas. They performed for U.S. troops across the country.

But when Demi entered middle school, things changed. There were some mean girls that made fun of her all the time. She hated it! Selena was there to support Demi, but those girls still made Demi sad. Demi even took a break from acting because she was so down. Finally, Demi decided to switch to homeschool.

She got back into acting and was happier than
ever. Demi did voice-overs for radio and
television commercials.

Next Demi had a small role on the Fox
series *Prison Break* in 2006. Then Demi landed
a role on Nickelodeon's *Just Jordan*. She had a
lot of fun on the set. It made her want to work
on more shows for kids her age. She just had
to keep auditioning until she found the perfect
show!

CHAPTER 3
SELENA TAKES ON DISNEY

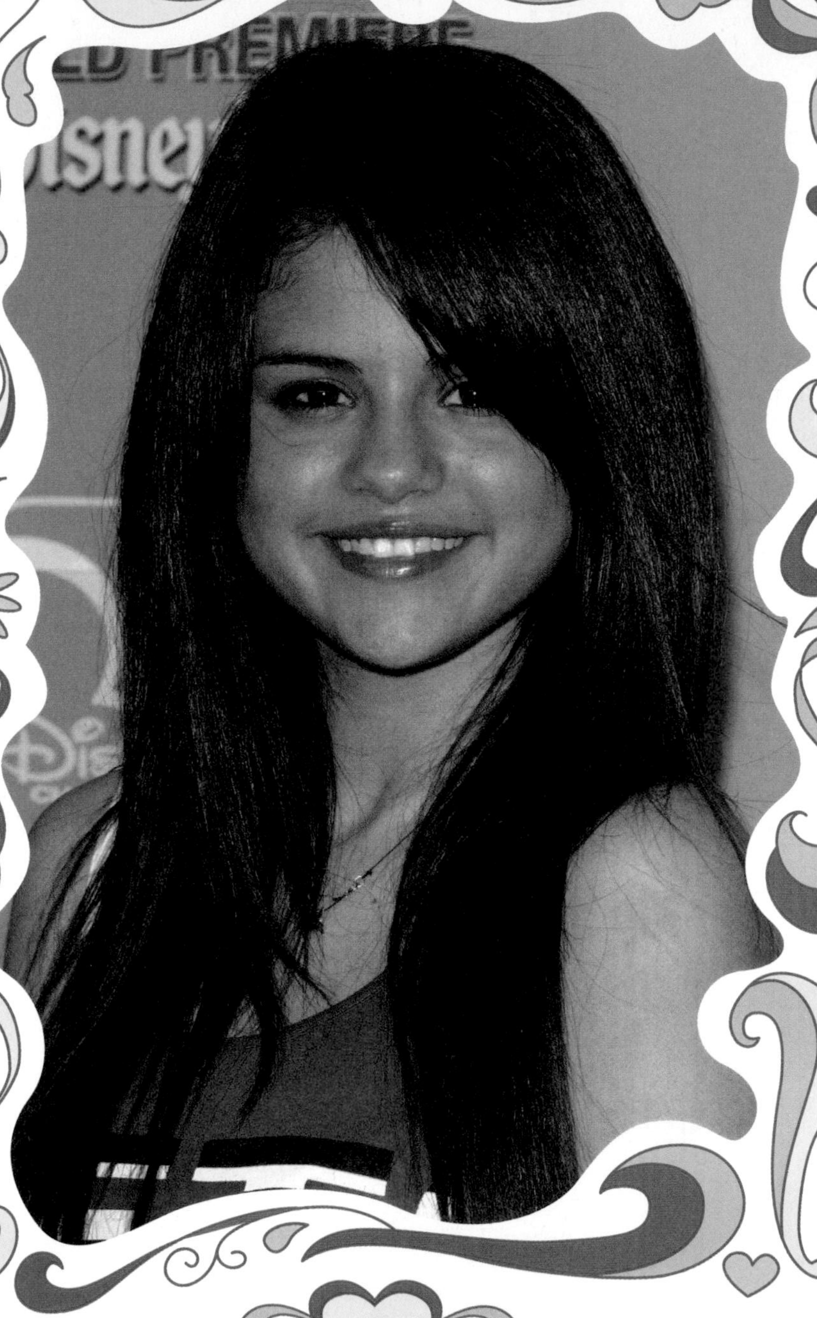

Selena was very excited to work with Disney. She just wished Demi could be there, too! Selena filmed three pilots for Disney. Only one of them made it on to TV. A pilot is an episode of a new show. Then television companies watch the pilots and pick which shows to put on TV.

Selena filmed pilots for shows called *What's Stevie Thinking*, *Wizards of Waverly Place*, and *Arwin!* Disney loved all three of the shows. But they decided *Wizards of Waverly Place* was the best. Selena and her family moved to Hollywood so Selena could begin filming. "It was sad to say good-bye to my friends and family, but it was a happy moment, too. They were so proud of me for achieving my dreams," Selena told *Discovery Girls* magazine.

Once she made the big move, Selena was excited to film her new show. But Disney wanted

her to do a few guest spots first. She filmed small parts on *The Suite Life of Zack & Cody* and *Hannah Montana*. Selena had a blast doing work for both shows. She made good friends with Cole and Dylan Sprouse and Brenda Song on *The Suite Life of Zack & Cody*. She also became friends with Miley Cyrus and

Emily Osment on *Hannah Montana*.

Then Selena got to work on her show. *Wizards of Waverly Place* is about the Russo family. The Russos live on Waverly Place in New York City. The family owns and runs a sandwich shop. They seem normal, but all three of the Russo kids are wizards! Selena's character is "Alex." Alex is sassy and likes to get into trouble. She is the only girl in the family. "I wanted to try something different, so I went in there and presented them with my way with Alex. She's very spunky. I didn't want her to be a kind of girly girl. So she's the very Converse-wearing, outgoing one, always getting in trouble and getting her brothers in trouble as well," Selena explained to the *Orange County Register.*

Selena was very happy with the rest of the cast. David Henrie plays Alex's older brother,

Justin, and Jake T. Austin plays the youngest Russo, Max. Jennifer Stone plays Alex's best friend Harper. David DeLuise plays their father, Jerry Russo, and Maria Canals-Barrera plays Theresa Russo, their mother. *Wizards of Waverly Place* became the first Disney series to ever feature a Hispanic family. The Russo family is Italian and Mexican.

Wizards of Waverly Place is definitely a comedy. The Russo kids aren't supposed to use their magic without their parents around. But Alex uses her magic all of the time. And it usually gets her in trouble. Luckily, her brothers are always there to help her! Of course, the magic and special effects on the show are very cool. They have spells for everything on the show. Alex can freeze time, make paintings come to life, and even make a double of herself!

Filming *Wizards of Waverly Place* has been really fun for Selena. She's become very good friends with David, Jake, and Jennifer. They like to hang out even when they aren't working. The three go surfing together at the beach. "I can't even explain it! I am very confident when I say that we are the closest cast Disney Channel has ever had. We've been told that because we spend every waking moment with each other—it's insane! Jake [Austin], Jen [Stone], David [Henrie], and I do karaoke together, we go to the movies, and we go surfing every weekend. And as soon as we get off work, we text and call each other. My mom is always like, 'You act like you never see each other!' We've just gotten so close." Selena told *Discovery Girls*.

Jennifer, Selena, and Jake take classes together before shooting every morning. Then,

in between takes, they do homework, talk, or play basketball. "We actually have one [a basketball court] on set. It's fun," Selena told *Girl's Life* magazine. Selena is pretty good at basketball. She can definitely beat her on-screen brothers!

Wizards of Waverly Place premiered on

October 12, 2007. It was a huge hit. Fans loved
the show so much that Disney quickly signed
the cast up for a second season. Then the cast
filmed an hour-long special that aired in April

2008. In the special, Alex and Justin go to summer school at WizardTech, a school just for wizards. The special was funny, exciting, and fans loved it. After that, Disney decided to film a real *Wizards of Waverly Place* movie.

In early 2009, Selena and the rest of the cast flew to Puerto Rico to film *Wizards of Waverly Place: The Movie*. The full-length Disney Channel Original Movie is set to air in late 2009. Selena told *MTV News* a little about what might happen in the film. "I think it would have to be that our secret is about to be exposed." So keep an eye out for the third season of *Wizards of Waverly Place* and the *Wizards* movie coming to a TV near you!

CHAPTER 4
Demi Joins the Family

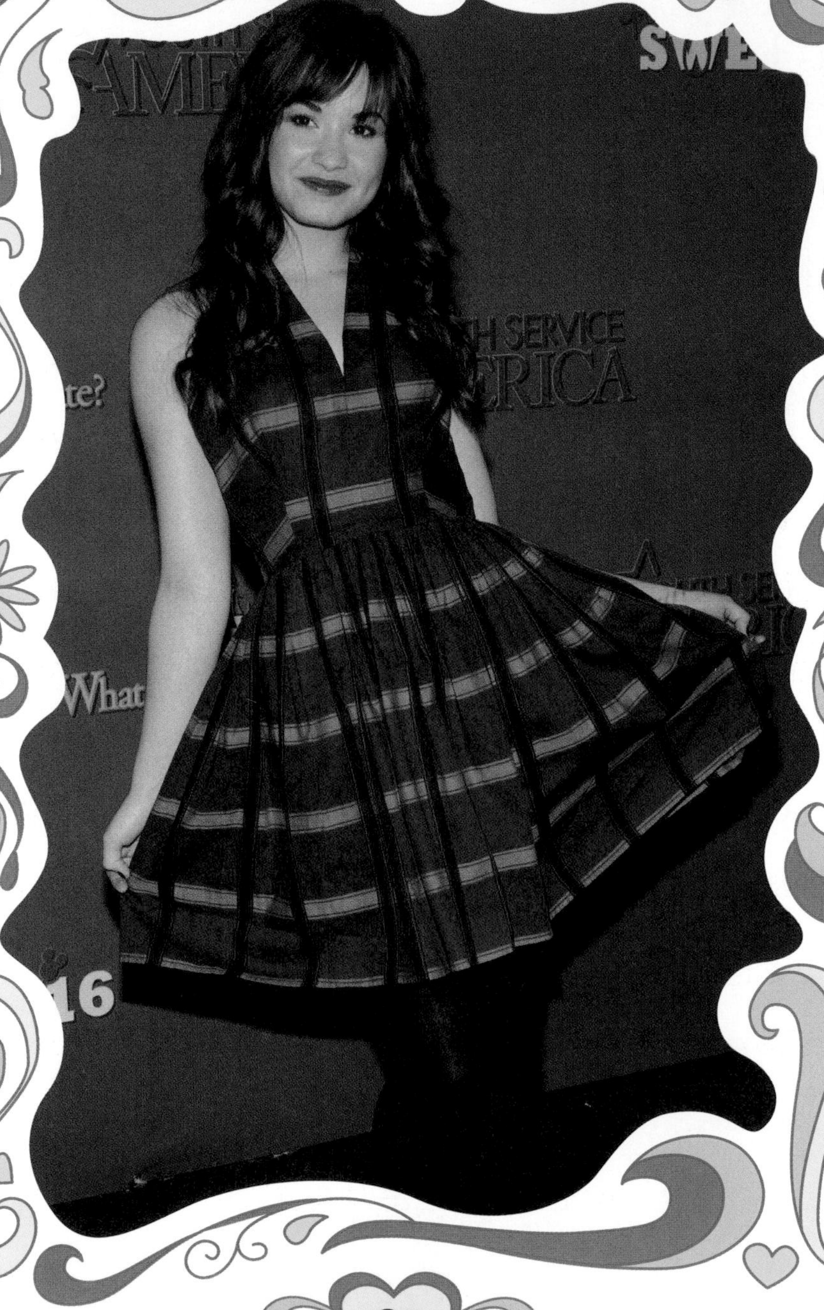

It was hard for the girls when Selena moved to Los Angeles. Selena was nervous working on her first show. She missed Demi's support. And Demi missed having fun with Selena on weekends. Luckily, they weren't apart for long.

Demi landed a role on a short Disney Channel series. The show is called *As the Bell Rings*, and each episode lasts five minutes. The show explores what happens in between classes at a middle school each day.

Demi was cast as "Charlotte." Charlotte is a pretty and talented musician—just like Demi! It was fun for Demi because she got to sing and act. The show is a comedy so there were lots of jokes and silly humor in the scripts. Demi told *Blast Magazine,* "It's awesome to do the show—very fast-paced and fun!" Of course, Demi did a great job.

Disney took notice. They invited her to

audition for other parts. Soon Demi was on her way to join Selena in Hollywood. Demi's first big Disney role was "Mitchie" in the made for television movie *Camp Rock*. Mitchie is a talented singer and songwriter who goes to a special camp for performers. Of course, Demi wasn't the only star of the movie. She was joined by the Jonas Brothers! The Jonas Brothers are one of the hottest bands in the world. Nick, Joe, and Kevin Jonas play the fictional boy band Connect 3 in the movie. Joe had the largest role of "Shane Gray," the lead singer of Connect 3 and Demi's love interest. Kevin played funny, silly "Jason," and Nick played serious, sensitive "Nate." Demi learned a lot from them about music and songwriting on the set.

Demi had a great time filming *Camp Rock*. She was very proud of the movie. It is all about being true to yourself. That was a message

Demi could really get behind! "It was a real confidence booster. My character and I both like to rock out and now we're not afraid to!" Demi told *Popstar!* magazine. Fans loved it too. The movie was a hit. Disney was quick to make a sequel. *Camp Rock 2* is set to debut in June 2009. It will include all of the original cast. We can't wait!

Next up for Demi was a Disney Channel television show. The studio developed a comedy just for her called *Sonny With a Chance*. It is about a girl named Sonny who gets cast on her favorite comedy show. Once Sonny arrives in

Hollywood, she has to juggle being an actress with being a regular teen. "I play Sonny, who's a girl from Wisconsin, and she kinda sticks out like a sore thumb, 'cause she's very quirky and very over the top," Demi told *MTV News*. "And she's, like, this little Midwestern or Wisconsin girl I kind of can relate to." Demi is new to Hollywood, too. So it was easy for her to get into character.

Sonny With a Chance is hilarious. Demi has dressed up like a bee, been covered in ketchup, and had her butt glued to a chair! And that's all only in the first season! Demi also has some great costars on the show, like cutie Sterling Knight and funny-girl Tiffany Thornton.

Sonny With a Chance was a big hit. So hopefully there will be more Sonny in Disney's future!

CHAPTER 5
BEAUTIFUL MUSIC

Both Demi and Selena are amazing actresses. But they have something else in common, too—they can both sing!

Selena has recorded a number of songs. She sang "Everything Is Not What It Seems." It's the theme song for *Wizards of Waverly Place*. She also recorded covers of several Disney classics like "Cruella De Vil" and "Fly to Your Heart." Next Selena recorded songs for a movie she was filming called *Another Cinderella Story*. These days, Selena's working on her own album. "I think you can be more of yourself when you're singing. . . . You write music and perform it, have fun, then go on concert and jam out in front of an audience." Selena told pbskids.org. Selena can't wait to go on tour. She would be especially excited if she could open up for her BFF Demi!

Demi is a few steps ahead of Selena in her

music career. Demi's songs from *Camp Rock* were a big hit. So Hollywood Records offered her a recording contract. Demi did a cover of "That's How You Know" from Disney's *Enchanted.* Then she recorded her debut album *Don't Forget.* Demi had already written some songs, but she worked with producers to make them perfect. The Jonas Brothers also helped her write new material!

Then Demi went on tour with the Jonas Brothers in the summer of 2008. Being on tour was a dream come true for Demi. "I know how excited I get when I go see concerts and people that I love. And I know every song of theirs. So to know that there are people in the audience that are excited to see me, it's still surreal," Demi told *TV Guide Online.* Fans loved Demi's album and it quickly rose to #2 on the Billboard Top 200 Chart. Demi was super

excited. It just made her more eager than ever to record more music for her fans!

Selena and Demi would love to go on tour together or even record a duet sometime soon! How cool would that be?

CHAPTER 6
YOUTUBE SENATIONS

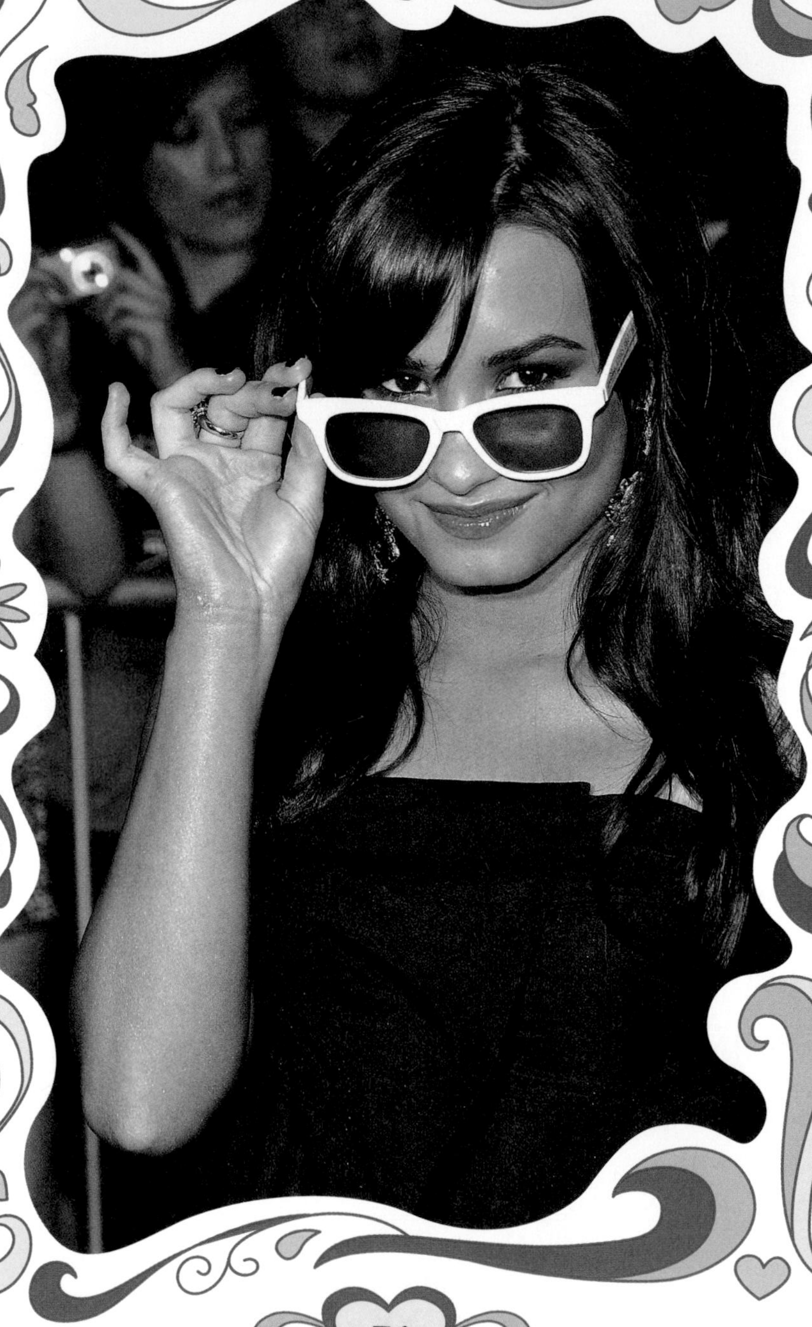

Selena and Demi always have fun together. They love shopping and watching movies together. They both love eating pickles and making Rice Krispies Treats. Both girls wished they could let fans see their awesome friendship, but they never got to work on the same movies.

Then, in January 2008, Demi had a great idea. She wanted to make videos with Selena and post them on YouTube on the Internet. Soon, the two girls were filming short funny videos wherever they went. They they put them up for their fans to see. They post their videos at http://www.youtube.com/user/therealdemilovato. A lot of the videos are silly and funny. The videos give fans a chance to get to know the real Demi and Selena. They plan to continue to make more videos as long as their fans keep watching them. So tune in whenever you can!

CHAPTER 7
movies!

Selena and Demi both love working on their Disney Channel shows. But they like to try other things, too.

Selena has done a lot of very cool projects. She provided the voice of "Helga" in *Horton Hears a Who!*, the animated film based on the classic Dr. Seuss story. "I had never done animation, so I thought it would be cool to try something different," Selena told the *New York Daily News*. Selena had a tough job. She played all 90 of the Mayor's daughters. And they were all named Helga! Selena had to come up with a voice for each. "I voiced all of them," Selena explained to the *New York Daily News*. "I had to change up my voice to do higher voices, and then bring it down to do lower voices. All of the Mayor's daughters look different, so I play many different characters."

Next up for Selena was the lead part of

"Mary Santiago" in *Another Cinderella Story*. The movie was a modern version of Cinderella. "At a ball, I meet a guy and we fall in love during a dance. Instead of dropping my glass slipper, I drop my MP3 player," Selena told the *New York Daily News*.

Selena's character is a dancer. Selena had to practice a lot for the part! She did a great job in the movie. She even sang a few songs for the soundtrack. *Another Cinderella Story* was released on DVD in late 2008 and premiered in ABC Family in early 2009. Fans loved the movie and were very impressed with Selena's dancing. Hmmm . . . maybe Alex Russo could do some dance moves on a future episode of *Wizards of Waverly Place*.

Selena's next role was extra exciting because of her costar. Selena would be starring as "Carter" in a new Disney Channel Original

Movie called *Princess Protection Program*. And Demi was starring as "Princess Rosie!" Selena and Demi were thrilled to work together again. They flew down to Puerto Rico to film the movie. In the movie, Princess Rosie is rescued from her country by Carter's dad. He is a secret agent of the Princess Protection Program. Carter

is a total tomboy and Rosie is a very proper princess. At first, the two don't get along. But then they start to learn from each other and they become friends.

Demi and Selena were psyched to be together for months! Demi told *Teen Magazine*, "Almost every scene we did, Selena would say, 'Oh my gosh, we're shooting a movie right now!'" The girls had hotel rooms right next door and spent all of their free time hanging out. They also made friends with the rest of the cast. Demi and Selena couldn't wait for their fans to see their movie. Hopefully they will get the chance to make a sequel or work together on another movie soon!

CHAPTER 8
BFF

Demi and Selena are still teens, but they are already big stars. And their futures are looking bright. They both plan to continue acting on their TV shows, auditioning for more movies, and working on their music. Demi is hoping to write all of the songs on her next album! And Selena is looking for cool movie roles. She will be playing "Beezus" in a film based on the children's book *Ramona the Pest*.

But no matter how famous Demi and Selena become, they will always stay best friends. Demi told *Teen Magazine*, ". . .We've been working at this for a really, really long time. We met each other the day we started working on [our careers] . . . It's been awesome." Of course, Demi and Selena will be there for each other in the future, too. Because life is always more fun with your best friend beside you!

SELENA GOMEZ

FULL NAME: Selena Marie Gomez

NICKNAME: Sel

BIRTH DATE: July 22, 1992

HOMETOWN: Grand Prairie, Texas

HEIGHT: 5'5"

PARENTS: dad Ricardo Gomez, mom Mandy Teefey and stepdad Brian Teefey

FAVORITE PIZZA TOPPINGS: mushrooms and jalepeños

FAVORITE SUBJECT: science

FAVORITE MOVIE: *Alice in Wonderland* and *The Wizard of Oz*

HOBBIES: singing, surfing, skateboarding

PETS: four dogs

DEMI LOVATO

FULL NAME: Demetria Devonne Lovato

NICKNAME: Demi

BIRTH DATE: August 20, 1992

BIRTHPLACE: Dallas, Texas

HEIGHT: 5'2"

PARENTS: dad Patrick Lovato, mom Dianna De La Garza, and stepdad Eddie De La Garza

SIBLINGS: older sister Dallas Lovato and younger sister Madison De La Garza

INSTRUMENTS: guitar and piano

FAVORITE CLOTHING: hats

FAVORITE FOODS: pickles, cheese, eggs, Rice Krispy treats, and chocolate

FAVORITE COLORS: red and black

HOBBIES: surfing, writing songs

To find out more about Demi and Selena, go online with a parent and check out these sites.

HTTP://WWW.YOUTUBE.COM/USER/THEREALDEMILOVATO

This is Selena and Demi's YouTube channel.

HTTP://WWW.SELENAGOMEZ.COM/

This is Selena's official Website.

HTTP://WWW.DEMILOVATO.COM/

This is Demi's official Website.